GETTING TO KNOW
THE U.S. PRESIDENTS

LYNDON B. JOHNSON

THIRTY-SIXTH PRESIDENT
1963 – 1969

WRITTEN AND ILLUSTRATED BY MIKE VENEZIA

CHILDREN'S PRESS®
A DIVISION OF SCHOLASTIC INC.
NEW YORK   TORONTO   LONDON   AUCKLAND   SYDNEY
MEXICO CITY   NEW DELHI   HONG KONG
DANBURY, CONNECTICUT

Reading Consultant: Nanci R. Vargus, Ed.D., Assistant Professor, School of Education, University of Indianapolis

Historical Consultant: Marc J. Selverstone, Ph.D., Assistant Professor, Miller Center of Public Affairs, University of Virginia

Photographs © 2007: Corbis Images: 3, 24, 27, 30 (Bettmann), 11, 18, 21; Getty Images: 29 (John Olson/Time Life Pictures), 31 (Three Lions/Hulton Archive); Library of Congress: 19; Lyndon Baines Johnson Library: 32 (Jack Kightlinger), 23 (Yoichi R. Okamoto), 25 (Cecil Stoughton), 13, 17; National Archives and Records Administration: 7.

Colorist for illustrations: Andrew Day

Library of Congress Cataloging-in-Publication Data

Venezia, Mike.
  Lyndon B. Johnson / written and illustrated by Mike Venezia.
    p. cm. — (Getting to know the U.S. Presidents)
  ISBN-13: 978-0-516-22640-8 (lib. bdg.)   978-0-531-17948-2 (pbk.)
  ISBN-10: 0-516-22640-1 (lib. bdg.)   0-531-17948-6 (pbk.)
  1. Johnson, Lyndon B. (Lyndon Baines), 1908–1973—Juvenile literature.
  2. Presidents—United States—Biography—Juvenile literature. I.
  Title. II. Series.

  E847.V46 2007
  973.923092—dc22
  [B]
                                                    2006023368

1 2 3 4 5 6 7 8 9 10 R 16 15 14 13 12 11 10 09 08 07

President Lyndon B. Johnson shows off his riding skills at his ranch in Texas in 1964.

Lyndon Baines Johnson was the thirty-sixth president of the United States. He was born near Stonewall, Texas, on August 27, 1908. Lyndon Johnson was John F. Kennedy's vice president. When President Kennedy was assassinated on November 22, 1963, Lyndon Johnson suddenly became president that day.

Lyndon B. Johnson, who was often called LBJ, started out as a really popular president. He kept the country together and running smoothly after a horrible tragedy. Lyndon carried out important programs that President Kennedy had dreamed of but never got the chance to accomplish. President Johnson helped pass civil-rights acts that made it against the law to keep African Americans from voting.

These acts also made it illegal to prevent people from eating at a restaurant or staying at a hotel because of the color of their skin.

On the other hand, Lyndon Johnson was responsible for sending thousands of American soldiers to fight a war in Vietnam. It wasn't long before the people of the United States grew to hate the war. When Lyndon Johnson left office, he was an extremely unpopular president.

Lyndon was born on a dusty ranch in the middle of Texas. His parents didn't have much money, but they showered their first son with love and attention. Mr. and Mrs. Johnson thought Lyndon was the most wonderful child in the world. Mrs. Johnson began to teach her son to read and write when he was only three years old.

It didn't take long before Lyndon believed he was the most wonderful child in the world, too. He became stubborn and unruly. Some neighbors even thought little Lyndon was a spoiled brat.

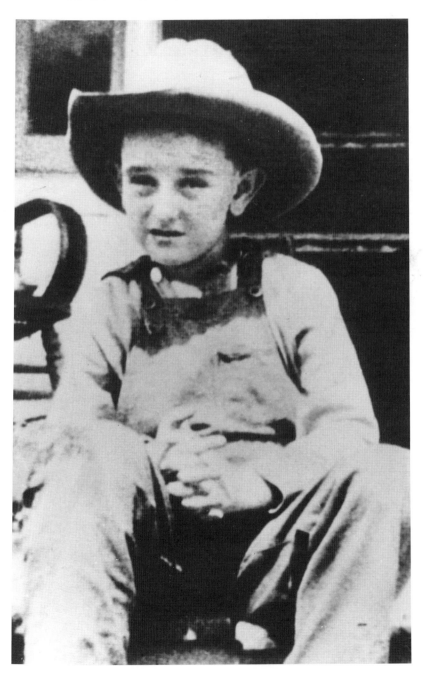

Lyndon Johnson at about the age of six

Lyndon started school in a one-room schoolhouse when he was four years old. He did pretty well in school. He was especially good at speaking and debating. Lyndon learned how to tell the best stories and really knew how to hold people's attention.

For years, Lyndon's parents and grandparents had told Lyndon exciting stories about their adventures as early Texas settlers. Some of the stories were more made up than real, but that didn't bother Lyndon at all. He learned to exaggerate many of his own stories, too.

While Lyndon was growing up, one of his favorite things to do was travel around Texas with his father in an old Model T Ford. Mr. Johnson was not only a farmer and rancher, but a member of the Texas state legislature. When it was time for elections, Lyndon was right there to help his father campaign.

Sam Johnson (left) and his son Lyndon (right)

Lyndon really looked up to his father. He dressed like him, walked like him, and loved politics just like him. At an early age, Lyndon Baines Johnson learned the importance of making friends and deals and keeping promises. Later he would use these skills as a politician.

Hangs around with bad kids

Crashes family car

Runs away

Gets into fight

After he graduated from high school in 1924, Lyndon got a job on a road-construction gang. Lyndon hated the job, though. He started to rebel and hang around with a bunch of wild kids. He once crashed his family's car, and then ran away from home because he was afraid of what his father would do.

Finally, after getting beaten up in a fight at a Saturday night dance, Lyndon decided to settle down and enroll in college. Mr. and Mrs. Johnson were thrilled! Lyndon got a good education at the Southwest Texas State Teachers College. He became an excellent teacher for a while, until he got an unexpected and exciting job offer.

In 1928, Lyndon Johnson (top row, center) taught at Welhausen School in Cotulla, Texas. Here he is shown with the athletic club he organized.

In 1931, a Texas congressman named Richard Kleberg heard about Lyndon's interest in politics. He knew Lyndon was a good teacher and hard worker. Congressman Kleberg asked Lyndon to come to Washington, D.C., with him and work as his assistant.

Lyndon couldn't wait! He spent the next three years discovering everything he could about how the U.S. government worked. Congressman Kleberg didn't seem to take his job very seriously. He often let Lyndon Johnson run his office, pretty much all on his own.

Once, on a trip home to Texas, Lyndon was introduced to a beautiful girl named Claudia Taylor. Claudia's nickname was Lady Bird because she was so pretty. Lyndon Johnson fell in love immediately. He was so crazy about Lady Bird that he asked her to marry him on their first date!

Lyndon and Lady Bird Johnson on their honeymoon in Mexico in 1934

At first, Lady Bird thought Lyndon was joking, but he was as serious as could be. Lyndon and Lady Bird got married less than three months later.

Lady Bird Johnson always helped her husband with his political career. Lyndon and Lady Bird eventually had two daughters, Lynda Bird and Luci Baines. Now everyone in the Johnson family had the same initials.

By 1935, Lyndon had made enough friends and connections in Washington, D.C., to help him get a special job in Texas. During the 1930s, the nation was suffering through the Great Depression, a time when many Americans lost their jobs and savings. Lyndon was put in charge of the Texas branch of the National Youth Administration. This program was one of many that President Franklin Roosevelt had created to help people find jobs.

A farm family during the Great Depression

National Youth Administration workers in Texas in the 1930s

Lyndon did an excellent job putting thousands of young people to work. When a special election came up to replace a U.S. congressman who had died, Lyndon decided to run for the spot. Lyndon had a reputation as someone who was hardworking and knew how to get things done. He won the election easily.

As a congressman, Lyndon was a loyal
Democrat who always supported Franklin
Roosevelt's programs to help needy people.
Lyndon was able to get bank loans for farmers
and low-cost housing for people in his district.
Lyndon was very proud to have brought
electricity to rural areas in Texas.

One area that got electricity for the first time was the hill country where Lyndon grew up. Now Lyndon's neighbors had power to pump water, light their houses, refrigerate food, and play radios. A few years later, Lyndon decided to run for the U.S. Senate. He lost his first race, but tried again in 1948 and won!

Johnson campaigning for the U.S. Senate in 1948

Most people agreed that Lyndon B. Johnson was a pretty remarkable congressman. Congress is the lawmaking branch of the U.S. government. Very often, members of Congress have a difficult time agreeing on which bills should be made into laws and which shouldn't. Lyndon Johnson was a genius at getting members of Congress to see things his way. He was even able to get Democrats and Republicans to work together. Sometimes, the 6-foot, 3-inch tall Lyndon would stand right in a person's face and poke him in the chest to get his attention.

Lyndon could scare some people into doing things his way. He could also make someone feel like a best friend and want to do things his way.

In 1955, Lyndon B. Johnson was elected majority leader of the Senate. This promotion made him one of the most powerful men in the nation. Five years later, Lyndon decided to run for president. The only problem was that the Democratic Party nominated John F. Kennedy instead. John Kennedy always respected Lyndon Johnson, though, and asked him to run as his vice president.

John F. Kennedy and Lyndon B. Johnson pose after being nominated for president and vice president

It was a close race, but Kennedy and Johnson won the 1960 election. Then, only three years later, President Kennedy was assassinated while visiting Dallas, Texas. That afternoon, Lyndon Baines Johnson was sworn in as the next president of the United States.

As Jacqueline Kennedy (right) looks on, Lyndon B. Johnson is sworn in as president of the United States.

Soon after he became president, Lyndon B. Johnson made a speech to tell the nation about his idea of a "Great Society." This program demanded an end to poverty and racial injustice in the United States. LBJ used all of his persuasive skills to get Congress together and pass laws to help the poor. Civil-rights acts were finally passed, too. Now minorities, especially African Americans, would be treated equally when it came time to vote, buy a house, or get a job. LBJ came up with plans called Medicare and Medicaid that helped older and poor Americans pay their medical bills.

President Johnson shakes hands with Dr. Martin Luther King Jr. after signing the Civil Rights Act of 1964.

LBJ seemed to be doing great. When it was time for the 1964 election, he won by a landslide! Things didn't stay great for long, though, because of a growing war in Vietnam. For years, the United States had been sending military advisors to help South Vietnam fight off Communist North Vietnam.

During this time, many Americans were worried about Communist governments taking over countries around the world. Communist governments were usually run by dictators.

These leaders ignored the human rights and freedoms of their citizens. President Johnson began sending thousands of troops to Vietnam to help the South. Except now, U.S. soldiers weren't acting as advisors. They were fighting the war.

Wounded U.S. Marines are carried away from battle during the war in Vietnam.

A peace demonstrator is knocked to the ground as he tries to break through police lines at a U.S. government building during an anti-war rally in 1967.

As more U.S. soldiers lost their lives in Vietnam, Americans began to protest against the war. It didn't seem like the United States had any business being there. LBJ didn't know what to do. He didn't want to lose a war against a tiny country like North Vietnam. Yet he realized that if the war continued, thousands more Americans would be killed.

Soon people were blaming President Johnson for killing American soldiers! This hurt him more than anything. At the same time, violent protests began to break out in African-American neighborhoods across the U.S. Many African Americans were still angry about the unfair way they had been treated for hundreds of years. They were also angry because money for helpful programs was being spent to support the war.

These people were protesting against the use of federal troops to control race riots in Newark, New Jersey, in 1967.

A sad, tired President Johnson listens to news about the fighting in Vietnam in 1968.

It was a troubling time in American history. President Johnson was blamed for most of the country's problems. When the next election came up in 1968, he announced that he would not run again. The story of Lyndon Johnson is a sad one. He really wanted to help people, and hoped to be remembered as America's greatest president. A terrible war had turned the country against him. In 1969, Lyndon and Lady Bird retired to their ranch in Texas. Lyndon died there five years later, on January 22, 1973.